D0829218

ARE YOU SICK OF BEING SICK?

MAYBE IT'S NOT YOUR ALLERGIES...

"WITHIN THE BODY THERE LIES A CURE"™

DR. KURT A. BARRETT

While the information in this book may be beneficial to patients, it is not to be interpreted as medical advice or consultation for any specific condition.

ISBN #0-9711719-0-4

Library of Congress Catalog #2001135625

Copyright 2002 by

Barrett Publishing
Battle Creek, Michigan

and

Dr. Kurt A. Barrett, D.O.

No portion of this publication may be reproduced, reprinted or otherwise copied for distribution purposes without the express written permission of the author and publisher.

All Rights Reserved.

TABLE OF CONTENTS

GENERAL PREMISE

The stomach normally makes hydrochloric acid to aid in digestion, however the acid becomes dangerous when it escapes up into the throat. Commonly prescribed medicines relieve heartburn and heal peptic ulcers. Higher dosages of these same medicines safely reduce acid even more, thus allowing our bodies to be freed of this burden of protecting the throat and lungs from the escaped acid. Wonderful things happen because "within the body there lies the cure."

PREFACE

GERD (Gastroesophageal Reflux Disease) is a common, chronic disorder characterized by the abnormal (pathologic) presence of acidic stomach contents in the lower food tube. I intend to introduce you to GERD and silent GERD. I have seen this condition in men and women from ages 2 to 101. You need to have certain basic facts to make sense of this disorder. Very strong (industrial strength?) hydrochloric acid is made by the lining of the stomach. The stomach is designed to protect itself from the acid. When acid escapes from the stomach into the esophagus (food tube) trouble begins. Our bodies recognize the inherent danger. We rally internal mechanisms to protect the esophagus and respiratory tract from the corrosive effects of the acid that has "escaped" from the stomach where it was made.* Heartburn is the most commonly recognized symptom. Approximately 20% to 40% of the western world experiences *DAILY* heartburn. People who have heartburn usually perceive this concept quite readily. The heartburn may respond to antacids, milk, food, or acid reducing medicines. Many people (over 50% of GERD patients) who have this unwanted occurrence of acid reflux *NEVER HAVE HEARTBURN*.

As many as 2/3 of the people who suffer from "sinus-allergy" problems (*especially* those who have failed conventional prescription and over-the-counter medicines) have some form of silent acid reflux related disorder. We call it silent because the

---

*Stomach acid routinely dissolves tin foil immediately on contact.

symptoms are not referable to the digestive tract. Their symptom relief with typical allergy-decongestant type of sinus medications is"so-so" at best. Based on history, physical signs, and symptoms, the diagnosis of GERD (even without heartburn) is suspected. The testing that we do to help us confirm this diagnosis is not especially accurate or easy to complete. This prompts us to suggest a therapeutic challenge. We use very safe, well tolerated medication that reduces the amount of hydrochloric acid that the stomach makes. If the person gets better it establishes the diagnosis. This therapy can make sinus problems disappear.

There can be several reasons for contents of the stomach to come in contact with the lower portion of the food tube. This unwanted occurrence stimulates our bodies to protect our delicate tissues. The lifestyle changes we use are aimed at reducing the exposure of the lower esophagus to regurgitated stomach contents. Raising the head of the bed, laying on the left side, avoiding late meals or evening snacks, reducing fat intake, weight reduction, elimination of caffeine, alcohol, and tobacco are all suggested.

I have asked you to read this, in an attempt to help explain why I am offering this treatment. If I only make one point, it is this; many patients with GERD *DO NOT HAVE HEART-BURN*. Some choke, sneeze, cough, or act just as if they had respiratory problems due to conventional causes. In reality these symptoms are demonstrating the body's built-in respect for the destructive qualities of our own homemade hydrochloric stomach acid. "Protect your easily injured tissues from this 'red hot' dangerous liquid," the brain screams out silently. The rest of the body, through the autonomic nervous system, responds. All you see are infections, mucous, congestion, and more as the result of being protected from an inevitable, catastrophic outcome, *IF THE ACID WAS LEFT UNCHECKED*. Hence, medicine that reduces the strength of stomach acid relieves the burden of protecting so fiercely when the gastric contents escape.

The results can be dramatic. Your body no longer has to function in such an ongoing state of emergency.

To get sinus relief, it appears necessary to reduce the acid content of the stomach's secretions more in some than in others. The antisecretory medicine we use may be less effective in certain people, resulting in the need for higher medication doses than traditionally used for heartburn control. We do not yet have therapies to fix the leak of acid from the stomach back into the esophagus. We make the substance that leaks less acidic, thus better tolerated. Finally you end up free from noxious symptoms and oftentimes astonished.

The medication is very specific in its action. It reduces the amount of hydrochloric acid your stomach makes. You do the rest; "within the body there lies a cure."

INTRODUCTION

Before you journey on for further information, I should tell you something about who I am. I graduated from Michigan State University, College of Osteopathic Medicine as a physician and surgeon in 1974. I came to Athens, Michigan and my current practice setting in 1977. I am board certified in Family Practice. I take pride in being a general practitioner. This rural, solo practice setting has permitted me to follow, first hand, many patients and families for over twenty years.

I truly love the intimacy and "smallness" of the solo practice of medicine. Our office policy is to treat each patient as I would want to be treated. I see each of my patients personally.

I am married and the father of four daughters. The women in my life have been extremely supportive, helpful, dedicated, and most of all, patient as I have explored the far reaching and sometimes devastating, effects GERD (GastroEsophageal Reflux Disease) has had on family, friends, and patients.

Look closely at the list of questions and ailments I deal with on a daily basis. I treat many patients who have long suffered from symptoms the medical community has been unable or reluctant to recognize as those of GERD. If you find yourself asking these questions and finding no relief, this book may offer an alternative. You could be feeling better than you have in a very long time. Your first step is to become educated on what GERD is and what it does. This may be the answer you have sought to feel better–**forever**! By reading this book you can better understand that within your body lies a cure.

DOCTOR WHY DO I:

Make so much mucous?

Have so many colds?

Have so much ear trouble?

Choke so easily, especially at night?

Have a runny nose all the time?

Have such a hard time finding any relief for my "allergies"?

Have so much sinus trouble?

Have dizziness?

Feel tired all of the time?

Just feel exhausted, and no one knows what's wrong with me?

Have trouble controlling headaches?

Have panic attacks?

Fill in the blank:

Dr., why can't I get my_____
under control?

Choose all that apply:

Abdominal Pain

Asthma

Back Pain

**Childs repeated and
prolonged ear infections**

Constipation

Cough

Diarrhea

Epstein Barr Virus

Hives

Hoarseness

Irritable Bowl Syndrome

Nosebleeds

Post Nasal Drip

Rectal Bleeding

SYMPTOMS AND FINDINGS OF GERD

GASTROESOPHAGEAL: Heartburn; chest, upper abdominal and neck pain; water brash (the taste of acid in the mouth or excessive saliva); belching; indigestion; nausea; vomiting and vomiting blood; painful swallowing or swallowing that causes food or pills to stick; halitosis (bad breath).

RESPIRATORY: Cough, wheeze, dyspnea (shortness of breath) or coughing up blood.

LARYNGEAL: Hoarseness, throat clearing, deep sighs associated with shortness of breath, soreness or irritation of the "Adam's Apple", voice changes, voice breaking, sensation of something stuck in the throat, excessive throat mucous.

PHARYNGEAL: Morning soreness or throat pain, gagging or choking, inability to brush the back of the tongue or rear teeth, sore throat.

NASAL: Congestion, itching, sneezing, soreness of the nose, post nasal drip, runny nose at mealtime.

SINUS: Headache, sinus pressure, pus-like discharge, facial pain.

OTIC: Ear pain, excessive drainage from the ears, hearing loss.

DENTAL: Loss of enamel, loss of teeth or multiple dental cavities.

DIFFICULT TO CONTROL: Blood pressure, asthma, snoring, sleep disturbance.

OTHER FINDINGS (UNCONFIRMED): Dizziness, back pain, joint pain, night time drooling, unusual skin rashes, hives, vision problems, erection dysfunction, frequent urination, night time urination, fatigue, depression, diarrhea, constipation, sweating, menstrual pain, menstrual clots, nose bleeds, tingling of the arms and legs.

ANATOMY

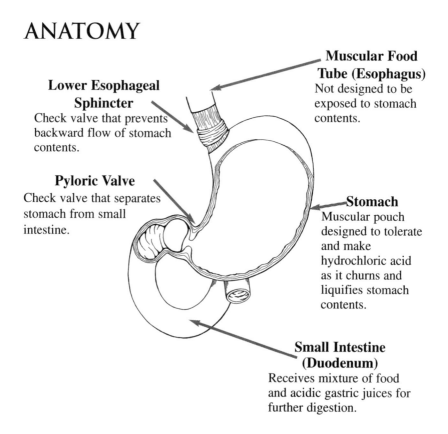

Muscular Food Tube (Esophagus)
Not designed to be exposed to stomach contents.

Lower Esophageal Sphincter
Check valve that prevents backward flow of stomach contents.

Pyloric Valve
Check valve that separates stomach from small intestine.

Stomach
Muscular pouch designed to tolerate and make hydrochloric acid as it churns and liquifies stomach contents.

Small Intestine (Duodenum)
Receives mixture of food and acidic gastric juices for further digestion.

NORMAL DIGESTION

Diaphragm
Muscular divider that separates the lungs above from
the abdomen below.

**Lower
Esophagus
Sphincter (#1)**
One way valve
allows passage
into the stomach.

Pyloric Valve (#2)
One way valve that allows
stomach contents to pass into
the duodenum (small intestine).

**Muscular
Wall of the
Stomach**

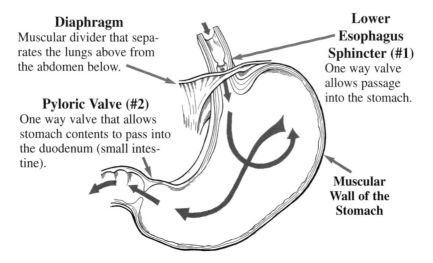

When food or drink enters the stomach via the esophagus, valve
#1 opens to allow entry, then closes to prevent reverse flow of
stomach contents. As part of digestion, valve #1 and #2 close and
the muscular stomach churns and mixes the stomach contents,
Partially digested liquid stomach contents (chyme) passes into
the small intestine as valve #2 relaxes.

Comments from Dorothy P.

My first problem with heartburn began during my pregnancy in 1969. My doctor suggested I use Rolaids, then Gelusil, but total relief came after the delivery of my son. I really didn't have any more problems unless I ate spicy or fatty foods. In the early 80s, I began having severe stomach pain, the doctor prescribed Tagamet, there was no indication of an ulcer and Tagamet relieved the pain. In 1989, I had my gall bladder removed; a stone was blocking the bile duct, causing a lot of discomfort.

In the early 90s, I began having heartburn, so again I used over-the-counter medications. Because of the stress of having a mentally ill daughter and job related stress, I did not see a doctor except for a regular yearly checkup, and the over-the-counter medications relieved my symptoms. In the early morning of April 15, 1996, I had severe chest pains. I had a stress test and nuclear imaging of my heart. The tests showed that everything was okay and I was advised that if I had any more pain, I should go to a doctor or emergency room as soon as possible. The problem was that the chest pains were erratic and short in duration, so I did not run to the doctor with every episode.

The checkup I had in 1997 did not explain the pain I was having recently in my pelvic area. The doctor referred me to a gynecologist, who after an examination, performed a laparoscopy and could see no problems. I was prescribed Elavil, which I refused to take–I did not feel my problems were in my head. At that point I changed doctors.

Doctor Barrett listened carefully to my history, ran tests with a heart doctor in Battle Creek. All tests were normal. My breathing problems were diagnosed as asthma, and medications were prescribed for sinus problems and possible allergies I was suffering from for years, and also Prilosec to alleviate the persistent heartburn.

During my routine yearly checkup in 2000, Dr. Barrett advised that he felt my problems to be related to GERD, which could be the source of my discomforts (chest pain, pelvic pain) all previously unexplained, as well as my asthma. The Prilosec had relieved my heartburn, and he felt that along with raising the head of my bed, following dietary guidelines, and increasing the dosage of Prilosec, the symptoms might all be alleviated. As unbelievable as it sounds, it worked.

With the symptoms gone, I reduced the dosage from 4 tablets a day to 1 in November 2000, feeling that one would be enough to control the problem. By May 2001, the chest and pelvic pains had returned. I spoke to Dr. Barrett about it and his further research with GERD led him to believe that I needed to increase the dosage again, as one tablet controls the heartburn, but does not keep the other symptoms at bay.

Currently all my symptoms have disappeared. I feel so much better, I have more energy, my outlook on life has changed to optimistic. Dr. Barrett continues to monitor the medications and my health in general. For so long I had felt that the doctors believed my problems to be in my head, and I was beginning to doubt my own sanity…especially in light of all the tests that were done in attempt to identify the pains and discomforts, with no definitive results. Today I feel that finally the diagnosis of GERD has identified the problem and the medications are working, thanks to a truly caring doctor who has been persistent in working to improve the health (mentally and physically) of one of many thankful patients. He could not be satisfied with just alleviating the symptoms, he kept working until the source was identified.

I
ACID RELATED DISORDERS (ARD)

GERD, a simple diversion from the normal state of health (specifically the movement of hydrochloric acid and stomach contents upward into the food tube) causes the body to protect itself and results in "sinus", "allergies", and other medical conditions. There is no recognized entity of GERD in non-industrialized countries. I wish I knew why.

Hydrochloric acid is one of the harshest, most chemically irritating substances there could possibly be. All people make hydrochloric acid. It's intended to aid digestion and be confined to the stomach except when it travels "downstream" where it is immediately diluted as part of normal digestion. Something in *our* industrially developed cultures causes our bodies to change. A one way muscular check valve at the stomach-esophagus junction is the barrier to regurgitation and is intended to contain acid within the stomach. It somehow fails to keep the acid where it belongs. The acid escapes upwardly, past the check valve into the esophagus. The esophagus was not designed for exposure to corrosive gastric contents. Our body very correctly interprets this as a clear and imminent danger. The afferent (input) portions of the autonomic nervous system perceives the dangerous nature of this acid located in a place where it is ***not supposed to be***. A very significant warning signal is generated. It tells the body to respond in a protective fashion. The tissues of the body respond through a variety of mechanisms including making mucous. The response mounted by the body takes the "edge" off the caustic nature of the regurgitated stomach contents. This reaction by the body tries to prevent the acid from traveling further from its point of origin. Depending on how your body reacts to this whole scenario **you may not have heartburn** or it may be mild or infrequent. It is not intuitive that something that happened the night before while you were asleep (regurgitation of stomach acid) results in problems the next day. As the stomach contents move up in the food tube one of the major dangers is contact with the extremely fragile and delicate tissues of the lungs. Most lay people and, a great number of health care professionals believe that this event (the movement of the stomach contents into the esophagus from the stomach) is heralded by heartburn. It often is, *but not in everyone all the time*! Historically we have believed that reducing the caustic nature of the regurgitated stomach contents, to the extent that relieves heartburn, is "good enough". I see this all the time. Patients and doctors alike treat only enough to keep heartburn under control. The more involved I have become in this issue of acid related disorders, the more perplexed I am by this style of thinking. Other, very troublesome problems are in want of resolution! This model of therapy is driven by traditional, widely disseminated guidelines for therapy. Medical professionals are repeatedly reminded to follow these recommendations. Deviation from this standard care demands labor intensive, time consuming justification. This makes professional life frustrating. I have a daughter who wouldn't be better if "traditional" guidelines for GERD with heartburn were adhered to.

The body can respond to this escaped acid in a number of ways: blood vessels are directed to leak like a sprinkler system; tissues weep to cause swelling; muscles are encouraged to squeeze and contract to the point of spasm; and an altered gummy, sticky mucus can be produced. All this in an effort to neutralize, trap, dilute, and absorb the dangerous stomach contents that have traveled up the esophagus from the stomach thru the faulty check valve. The body perceives this as such an immediate danger that it diverts its limited resources away from other health issues. The demands placed on the finite resources our body has to protect the esophagus, and respiratory tract can use up our "metabolic energy". There are studies that show alterations of the reticulo-endothelial system (the immune system) and this represents a very serious consequence. The body's defense mechanisms can only protect against a certain number of insults at any one given time. It's as if the body makes a priority list of what and just how dangerous these insults are. It also appears that reflux of stomach contents, moving in the direction of the respiratory tract, is extremely high on the list of things that need to be protected against. In doing this, the body seems to ignore, or is unable to cope with, other less immediate, although extremely significant insults.

A pH scale is a "thermometer of acidity". The scale goes from 0-14, 7 is neither acidic, nor basic, but "neutral". Stomach acid routinely measures below 2.0 on this scale, thus making it *extremely* acidic. Because we make acid during the night time hours, people may awaken in the morning with their most profound symptoms. Unless they encounter other irritating events, they sometimes get better as the day goes on. Their symptoms *may* become less troublesome. This is not always the case by any means. It is harder for the acid to "climb" the esophagus when you are up and around all day than it is when you lie down at night because of gravity. However, some occupations and activities seem to predispose to this daytime reflux. One example is long haul truck drivers. They spend a great deal of time sitting, often with a belt that acts like a cinch. This gives a "tourniquet effect" to the bowel which causes a low grade obstruction to the flow of intestinal contents. The end result is a large percentage of truck drivers with GERD.

Bending over at the waist can act the same way. One elderly patient recently caused an episode of sinus problems. She was picking strawberries, something she would not ordinarily do, but her husband was too ill to pick them. She would use her cane as a support, placing it firmly against her upper abdomen and then bend at the waist because of arthritic knees and ankles. The cane thus pressed against her stomach while she picked strawberries. It didn't cause any abdominal pain or heartburn. It made her believe she had contracted some type of sinus trouble. In fact, she was forcing the stomach contents up into the food tube with her posture. Her body made the mucous in the sinuses because of the "close connection" to the esophagus. All this as an automatic reflex to protect herself from the dangers of the stomach contents being forced up the food tube toward the respiratory tract. The end result was sinus trouble. No gastrointestinal complaints at all. Treat her stomach acid regurgitation and the sinus problem disappears.

Another lady is in complete remission from GERD and sinus symptoms except when she plays golf. "There is something on the golf course that makes my eyes water, my nose runs and I cough. I must be allergic to something there." It turns out that she is not allergic or coming in contact with sensitizing chemicals or other external substances that caused her to produce the mucous. It was what she *does* while she is on the golf course. Bending over at the waist to handle the golf ball causes the retrograde flow of stomach contents into the esophagus (*no* heartburn mind you). The body is protecting her from this acid reflux by making mucous. Not just by making mucous in the esophagus, but in the ears, nose, throat, and elsewhere.

GERD is a problem that runs in families. In my experience there is rarely just one family member involved. This is an extremely common condition that affects millions of Americans. The first step in solving a problem is recognizing that a problem exists. Right now, until we get a better concept about why gastric contents escape so frequently, therapy that helps the majority of people is reducing the harshness of the stomach acid. This doesn't "cure" everyone because there are different reasons why people regurgitate stomach contents. The proton pump inhibitors (Prilosec, Prevacid, Aciphex, Protonix, and Nexium) are all very closely chemically related. These medications are non-toxic, extremely well tolerated, and appear to be very mild in terms of side effects. The overwhelming majority of authorities agree that these medicines are not only effective, but extremely safe, both long and short term.

One has to consider the potential consequences of untreated acid reflux disorders. Untreated GERD, as medicine understands it now, rarely causes immediate life threatening consequences. It can claim lives when it results in bowel hemorrhage, scar tissue of the lungs, intractable asthma, recurrent pneumonia, cancer of the voice box, and more. Mostly GERD makes people miserable and adversely effects the quality of life. It's a chronic disease. Each day, people awaken after being "under attack" by their own secretion, hydrochloric acid. Some days are worse than others. Oftentimes, how miserable they are depends on what happened in their esophagus the night before.

Sleep disturbances can cause GERD and conversely GERD can also cause sleep disturbances. Beware that sleep apnea associated with GERD, can be either a cause or a result. There appears to be an unusually high incidence of gallbladder problems associated with GERD. Gallbladder disease can cause GERD symptoms. Likewise, the GERD mechanics can result in gallbladder disease.

GERD does not discriminate by age, race, or gender. The youngest patients I have successfully treated are around two years old and the oldest have been over one hundred.

Typical symptoms in some GERD patients are complaints about the *kind* of mucous they make. It is so sticky that they feel as if they have to reach into the back of their throats and literally pull the mucous out. Some of this sensation is caused by swelling of the throat tissues in conjunction with this special thick, dense, sticky, adherent mucous.

If your mother didn't tell you, "nothing smaller than your elbow in your ear," she should have. Cotton swabs can easily damage the ear canal. GERD patients have an unusual propensity to feel the necessity to aggressivley clean their ears, often with cotton swabs after they shower. This is strictly forbidden, instead they might try a few drops of rubbing alcohol in the ear to evaporate the water. In these individuals, the ear canal is already swollen and hence, hypersensitive. They can't stand anything (water) in the canal of the ear so they "go after it".

People who say, "I can't swallow pills. I'll gag," are almost always GERD patients. After a few days of GERD therapy they often can swallow any size pill.

Halitosis in my patients is exclusively related to GERD. Halitosis is not the result of poor oral hygiene. It is a result of making excessive mucous which clings to the teeth and hence allows bacteria to grow. Bacterial growth results in this characteristic odor. The mucous is so adherent to the teeth that they are unable to brush it away no matter how often and how hard they try. Only a small minority of GERD patients have halitosis. Every halitosis patient I have ever seen I believe had GERD. The same goes for that person at the water cooler who always "sniffs" and clears their throat. They almost always have GERD. I say that because they have usually been treated and on their own have tried numerous remedies without relief.

If you are doing your own research, key words are: acid reflux, laryngotracheal reflux, gastro-esophageal reflux, gastric reflux, esophageal reflux, esophagitis, hiatal hernia, GER, NERD, non-erosive reflux disorder, extra-esophageal manifestations of GERD, atypical symptoms of GERD, silent GERD, and GERD.

Dr. Andrew Taylor Still, M.D. D.O., Civil War surgeon founded Osteopathy over 100 years ago on the belief that the body can heal itself. I understand this concept more clearly since I have seen spectacular outcomes from treating GERD. When wayward acid is reduced or contained the body says, "Thank you for helping". The activated protective mechanisms are no longer engaged and a state of health ensues. This quality of life can be truly remarkable. As a result of moderating the stomach acid, I have had people comment, "This is the best I have felt in 10, 15, 20 years or more." There is more here through GERD and the autonomic nervous system than just sinus and respiratory problems. Many other troublesome symptoms (diarrhea, constipation, rectal bleeding, fatigue, recurrent infections, joint pain, and the list goes on) resolve; often for the first time in a person's memory, through the treatment of silent GERD.

The normal state of the body is a state of health. Something about western civilization with industrialized societies results in this phenomenon of acid related disorders (ARD). I don't know what initiates this process, but I certainly would like to find out. Research on this topic through Michigan State University is being assessed as we go to print. These ARD's plague a huge number of people as manifested by the first proton pump inhibitor, Prilosec, being the number one prescribed medication in the United States. One capsule of any strength proton pump inhibitor is ***usually enough to relieve heartburn***. There is more to the story than just heartburn. Remember that this most common prescription medication in the United States is being used to relieve heartburn. The **majority** of people that have this condition have never had heartburn or never consider their heartburn serious enough to treat. Heartburn *IS NOT* normal. Since it occurs so commonly, it appears to be a consequence of life in our current environment. Even though millions of people in the United States suffer from heartburn every day, it should not be regarded as "just one of those things". I would like to add here that these medications, the proton pump inhibitors, are superb at healing peptic ulcer disease. They are so effective, along with other newer techniques (like eradicating Helicobactor-pylori bacteria with antibiotics) that peptic ulcer disease is actually becoming rare. It will soon be "retired" to take its place in the archives of medicine alongside smallpox, diphtheria, and other infectious diseases.

A German philosopher once said "The eyes only see what the mind knows". I truly believe that the future of improved health will be thru better understanding of particularly silent, atypical, supra-esophageal manifestations of GERD (NERD) or what we may end up someday calling SNERD (silent non-erosive esophageal reflux disorder).

Sir William Osler, one of the greatest physicians of all time, noted the relationship between ASTHMA and a DISTENDED STOMACH *over one hundred years ago*! It's high time we followed up on his observations because **within the body there lies a cure**.

II
DR. BARRETT, WHY DO
YOU KNOW ABOUT THIS?

The whole subject of respiratory and allergy problems has been a rather personal issue. My mother was plagued by severe asthma throughout her adult lifetime. The primary reason I became involved in these fascinating conditions, however, has to do with another family member, my oldest daughter. As you will soon see, it's her "fault" that I became so intensively involved in this area of medical care.

She had ear, nose, and throat problems with a tendency to experience choking, gagging episodes throughout the years. The allergist tested her and reported she was allergic to dust mites. This seemed a reasonable answer. The usual allergy medications and control measures were initiated, but her symptoms were *never* successfully eradicated. This went on for 15 years and a half dozen doctors.

Several years ago, when she was home from college, we went for a walk. It was a cold blustery Michigan day, typical for Thanksgiving time of year. The exposure to the cold air precipitated respiratory irritation and "asthma like" symptoms of cough, choking, and gagging. "I can't catch my breath, we have to go back to the house," she insisted. Her symptoms alarmed me.

As a result of her respiratory problems during our walk, my daughter and I went straight to my Athens, Michigan office to evaluate her for what I believed to be a form of asthma.

I was unable to demonstrate any evidence of asthma. Nevertheless, we tried to use asthma/allergy type medications. The results were dismal. I was baffled. I watched and listened intently to the various characteristics of her signs and symptoms. I perceived the origin of her problem to be from her esophagus. I was puzzled as to the relationship between symptoms of the cold air and her esophagus and at this point consulted with a stomach and bowel specialist (gastroenterologist). This was several years ago and I was assured that in the absence of heartburn there was no possibility whatsoever of this problem originating in her food tube. This threw me off track for years.

Fast-forward several years. My daughter called and asked, "What can I do for my heartburn?"

In all her years of what I had perceived to be an esophageal problem, she had never had heartburn, not even once. This was the "break" in her saga that allowed me the courage to believe she was, in fact, having problems with her esophagus, even though symptoms were almost exclusively respiratory in nature. If I could learn more about the esophagus, I might be able to alleviate her choking episodes. I started to "Dig On." [1]

I immediately began to read every article I could find on the esophagus and reflux. It became readily apparent that my daughter (and an enormous number of others) possessed some connection between respiratory symptoms, asthma, sinus trouble, runny nose, cough, excess mucous, choking, headaches, nose bleeds, hoarseness, gagging, etc. and the regurgitation of the stomach contents into the esophagus. Paradoxically, the majority of these people rarely or never have heartburn as a clue. Their bodies' protective response to the escaped acid is so effective that classic GERD symptoms are absent.

Dr. Joel Richter, professor of medicine and chairman of the department of gastroenterology at Cleveland Clinic Foundation is an expert in this area. Dr. Ronnie Fass at the University of

---

[1] The Osteopathic concept to "Dig On" is synonymous with the "old time" philosophy of the Doctor of Osteopathy to pursue the *true* cause–hence, if you influence the cause, the "effects" vanish. They claimed D.O. stood as much for "Dig On" to find the cause as it did for <u>D</u>octor of <u>O</u>steopathy.

Arizona is also researching GERD without heartburn. Literature they have authored has guided me in my approach to treatment and diagnosis. Cleveland Clinic has an ongoing joint clinical program involving the departments of gastroenterology, otolaryngology and communicative disorders. "Voice" patients were found to frequently have GERD, often without heartburn. They have to treat GERD to get their voices better.

Both Dr. Richter and Dr. Fass have endorsed high dose therapy with proton pump inhibitors. Their guidelines for cough and chest pain have served me well in an attempt to diagnose and treat first my daughters and now many of my patients. By using GERD treatment for respiratory symptoms, I have found wonderful outcomes to more problems than I ever *dreamed* possible.

Case Study

A 54-year-old female with a long standing history of allergic conjunctivitis (pink eye), uncontrolled by medicines and eye drops during previous allergy seasons. The outcome: GERD therapy initiated even though the patient was skeptical since she had never had any form of GI distress. Within a month of initiating therapy she stated, "I feel more like myself now." She experienced upset stomach and minor side effects with two different kinds of proton pump inhibitors. She continued therapy in spite of this. In reference to the recent allergy season, her report is: "The best allergy season I have ever had. I feel like my allergies are totally gone. I think I used 1 eye drop once this year and I didn't require any allergy pills or nose spray." She remains in remission.

Case Study

A 50-year-old male with a long history of severe respiratory problems and shortness of breath. He has seen numerous specialists through the years. I received a phone call from his wife in 1996 indicating "something has to be done he gags and chokes and can't breath. He has repeated respiratory infections." The patient "demonstrated" to me symptoms of GERD by opening his mouth and pointing with his index finger toward the back of his throat and saying, "the problem is right here I can't get the phlegm past this point". Despite conventional therapy resolution of symptoms was limited and repeated infections and chronic shortness of breath persisted. Finally in May of 2000 heartburn surfaced and he was started on proton pump inhibitor therapy. At this point he is not just better he is dramatically improved. His exercise tolerance has improved he doesn't cough and raise morning secretions. His wife reports, "I am shocked. He is 100 fold better than he has ever been before!"

III
WHY CAN'T
I GET BETTER?

Another of my daughters, who now lives on the East Coast, has had serious sinus problems, repeated sore throats, and attacks of severe hives since kindergarten. Interestingly, her hives were precipitated with exposure to cold air. Over the years, she has seen a number of specialists and general doctors who have all suggested she continue treating her symptoms with antihistamines and avoid exposure to the cold when possible. Though she had repeatedly searched for relief from symptoms that plagued her, no one seemed to have the answer to what was causing these problems.

Recently I received a phone call from her. She had just come from another allergist's office.

"They just don't know what I am allergic to and I am sick of being sick!" she exclaimed in exasperation.

My response to her dilemma was a question.

"Do you have heartburn?" I asked.

When she responded that on occasion she did have heartburn I immediately suggested therapy completely different from anything she had ever tried before. I recommended prescription strength acid blocking capsules twice a day to help reduce the intensity of the acid made by her stomach.

Her symptoms, of sinus problems and severe allergies, were actually symptoms of GERD and were being caused by the escape of the stomach acid produced by her own body.

The strong acid her stomach manufactured was coming in contact with her food tube where it joins the stomach, thus, causing her body to produce, through internal automatic reflexes, large amounts of mucous in a *successful* attempt to prevent damage to the delicate lining of the food tube. The mucous protected her, but at the same time, made her miserable.

By taking the prescription acid blocking capsules, the strength of the stomach acid my daughter's body was producing was reduced (we never eliminate the production of stomach acid with any acid reducer medication). Her body no longer felt the need to protect itself from the milder, less damaging stomach acid.

Three weeks later her symptoms were gone. For the first time in her memory, she was relieved of unwanted phlegm, nasal congestion, sneezing, sore throat, and cough. The result: no respiratory infections, excess mucous production, wheezing or hives. She no longer was susceptible to contracting each infection she came into contact with. ***Her allergy symptoms disappeared.***

Over the years, all of the nasal sprays and antihistamine decongestant combinations we tried failed her. She had tested in the past for allergies on numerous occasions to no avail. It looked and acted like allergy should. The reason no one was successful in pinpointing her "allergy" is because allergies weren't really the problem triggering her illness. Reducing the intensity of acid in her stomach resolved her "sinus/allergy" trouble. She is remarkably better and can be expected to continue to do well in the future now that we know the source of her problems.

This very safe, extensively tested, well tolerated, but expensive ($3.00 or more per capsule in 2001) medication, taken on a daily basis, has resulted in complete eradication of my daughter's symptoms.

Case Study

A 6-year-old female had a long standing history of ear infections, throat clearing, and chronic ear pain. Therapy with acid blockers was initiated. At follow up her mom report that she has noticed a dramatic change–the child's failure to awaken 1 to 1-1/2 hours after going to bed with a stomach ache (she used to give her Pepto Bismol). She has found that it is no longer necessary. She also notices the absence of sneezing or coughing and no further ear problems. The child states "I just feel a little bit better." Initially mom was skeptical of the results so she withheld the medication and the symptoms all returned. When she reinstituted the medication, the symptoms went into total remission and remain in remission.

Case Study

A 12-year-old boy with complaints of long standing ear problems, nasal congestion, unusual skin rashes and joint pain. The family history is positive for GERD. Medication was instituted along with the elevation of the head of the bed and dietary measures. Total resolution of joint pain, skin rash, respiratory congestion and episodes of ear pain were achieved. The child states, "I feel more awake now." He continues on proton pump inhibitors.

IV
WHY DO I ALWAYS COUGH?

Lynn (names have been changed) a woman in her 40's, appeared in my Athens, Michigan office with a history of a chronic cough.

"I have been coughing for almost ten years," she explained to me. "I have asthma."

Lynn had good resources for medical care on her behalf and had experienced thorough evaluations. Despite treatment for asthma by pulmonary specialists, she continued to cough.

Through associates at work, Lynn was familiar with the basic concept that I had been promoting. Reducing stomach acid may relieve her cough. She took the information to her pulmonary specialist. He agreed to let her try this therapy. Within three weeks of starting acid blocking medication, she was completely free from coughing for the first time in years. With ongoing adjustment of her dose and continued management of her medical care, Lynn has not only resolved her cough, but has gone on to continued improvement of her health in other areas that would have seemed unrelated to the casual observer.

I saw her recently at the office and she reported, "I have stopped all asthma medications on my own. I don't need them anymore. I haven't had a single wheeze or cough. The month of May is always the worst and it didn't bother me a bit this year, even *without* asthma medication!"

Case Study

37-year-old male presented initially with a ruptured right ear drum. Antibiotics, decongestants and ear drops relieved the acute phase but the disruption of the ear drum persisted. GERD therapy was instituted and within 72 hours the patient reported dramatic reduction of long standing joint and neck pain as an unexpected benefit of this therapy. He has gone on to resolve the ruptured ear drum with resolution of the mucous production and long-term remission of neck and joint pain (he was told 20 years ago that pain would be with him the rest of his life as a result of an automobile accident).

Case Study

A 15-year-old male with dizzy spells, headaches, excess respiratory mucous and a 10 year history of allergic skin rashes (eczema). He previously treated with prescription allergy sprays with modest relief from the nasal inhaler but didn't like the odor. Family history of GERD. Outcome: Therapy initiated with follow-up at three weeks at which time the 15-year-old states, "As far as I am concerned, I am all better. This is the first time that I haven't had a rash on my arm in 10 years. By 7 to 10 days the rash was gone." The dizziness is gone, headaches are gone and when asked if there was anything else different, he responded, "It seems like I am able to concentrate better. In the past when I would read something, when I looked away to copy it I would have to look back to remember it, and now I can write it down the first time, every time." He remains in total remission on proton pump inhibitor therapy as well as life style modifications.

V

OH, IT'S JUST MY ALLERGIES... OR IS IT?

(THINGS ARE NOT ALWAYS AS THEY SEEM)

Forty-one-year-old Sam came to my office with the complaint, "I've had sinus trouble all my life. Nothing has ever worked. What do you have to help me?"

Sam's history and physical examination suggested that he had respiratory allergies. He was placed on a prescription nasal spray to control allergies and asked to return in one month.

At the time of his re-check, he was ecstatic. In his own words, he was "perfect."

"I even drove all the way to Florida and back. I only sneezed twice!" he said excitedly.

To him it was unbelievable that he could possibly have such a simple resolution to this long-standing problem by spraying an inhalation of vaporized medication into each nostril *once daily*. This treatment *totally* relieved his suffering. Sam's sinus problems are now a thing of the past. The modern allergy medications we have are so wonderfully effective that complete resolution of symptoms is what I expect. If you don't respond like Sam then something else is contributing to your symptoms.

A similar situation *seemed* apparent when a gentleman of the same age experienced recurrent problems with respiratory infections and ear pain. He also had a long-standing history of profound "hay fever" symptoms during the harvesting of the hay crops. Despite trying all available allergy medications, Herman found it necessary to carry a roll of paper towels on the tractor. Commencing with the first pass around the hayfield, his eyes would begin to water, his nose would run, and he would begin to sneeze to such an extent that he would go through a whole roll of paper towel.

It was his experience that allergy medication was of no benefit in controlling or preventing these symptoms. Since this was a chronic issue, the failure of the medications to help him with this problem had caused him to be completely discouraged about medical care in general.

He arrived at my office with an entirely different complaint from hay fever symptoms; that of strangling at night and bolting upright in bed to catch his breath. Herman had already exhausted all options and resources at his disposal with no relief. After examining him and reviewing his history, it appeared likely that he was experiencing acid reflux at night (the unwanted movement of stomach contents into the food tube, especially when lying down). He was placed on proton pump inhibitor capsules twice a day and showed a truly remarkable response with normalization of his sleep. No more dreaded nighttime choking spells. The added benefit was complete relief of ear, nose, and throat problems. In addition, he mowed all three cuttings of hay and not once required so much as a single Kleenex, eye drop, or had a solitary sneeze!

The clear implication is that his body's response (in order to protect him from the escaped stomach acid) was so dramatic, so profound, that reducing the stomach acid intensity not only relieved the nighttime choking episodes, but at the same time, *eradicated* his sensitivity to inhaled allergens. His hay fever went away completely. His ear pain, sinus headaches, and nasal congestion were resolved as well. You see, his symptoms were caused by GERD, *not* by "allergies".

These long standing problems, which appear allergy-like in nature, have been caused by the body protecting itself from the escaped gastric contents. The mucous protects people from their *own stomach acid.* The body, through the autonomic ("automatic pilot") nervous system, does its job of protecting against injury to the food tube and lungs. In the end, the person deals with mucous where they don't really want mucous. All this to protect yourself from the harmful effects of "wayward" hydrochloric acid generated by the stomach to aid in digestion.

People often **assume** they have sinus problems caused by allergies. Herman has come to realize that his symptoms can be controlled if the correct diagnosis is established and treated intensively. Obviously air quality played a huge role in the development of symptoms while he mowed hay. When the underlying GERD symptoms are brought under control, his body responds to the air quality issues in an entirely different manner, one that is appropriate. This indicates that allergies play little if any role in his problems. Treat allergies and he has no relief; treat for GERD and *all* his symptoms resolve.*

Commercial advertising influences us into thinking that allergies are the sole or primary cause of rhinitis and headache. The antihistamines and various allergy remedies that we are exposed to in television and magazine ads are wonderful medications and are really miracle drugs. However, they only work if the underlying problem is allergy induced. After being given a trial of allergy medications, people often come back with one of two responses. If they do have pure respiratory allergies, they proclaim any of the modern prescription antihistamines or nasal sprays to be miracle cures. I often hear them say, "Doc, this is the best I've ever been!" The second response (unfortunately this tends to be in the majority) is, "Maybe it helped. I am not sure. Perhaps I am a little better, but I can't really tell." At this time, I immediately become suspicious. Something else is at work here. There is no point in using more or different allergy medicine.

A recent study by a large company that employs one of my patients tested 200 workers on a *voluntary* basis for allergy related problems. Bradley, my patient, volunteered for the blood test because he had chronic sinus problems. The test is called an

---

*Some patients will have both GERD and respiratory allergies and need both conditions treated for complete symptom relief.

immunoglobulin E level (IgE). This test is considered nearly 100% accurate for detecting the presence of respiratory allergies. It does not tell you what you are allergic to; it only confirms or denies the existence of respiratory allergies. Despite Bradley's sinus complaints, he tested negative for IgE blood levels. This indicates that his sinus problems **ARE NOT** the result of allergies to pollen, animal dander, dust, dust mites, etc. Now, for the really interesting part. Of these 200 people most assumed they had respiratory allergies. Two thirds tested **NEGATIVE** on the IgE blood test. No respiratory allergies in them. This means that only *one* in *three* have even a chance to respond to allergy remedies. My patient has responded to GERD therapy and his sinus problems are dramatically improved. Even though the symptoms may be exactly the same, please remember this one fact: **ALL SINUS PROBLEMS ARE NOT CAUSED BY ALLERGIES.** If you have treated and treated and treated, you can continue to treat some more, but until you have treated the real cause of your problem, you won't get well. Incidentally, the same goes for headaches. Direct to consumer advertising would have us believe that over the counter and prescription remedies (usually antihistamines, decongestants, and pain relievers, often all in one capsule or tablet) are the answer for "sinus headache". We have been "brainwashed" by Madison Avenue into believing these assumptions are fact. Believe me, this is not fact.

Here is what I call the flat tire syndrome. All flat tires look the same. Just because the last flat tire was the result of a leaky valve stem does not mean the next flat tire will be caused by the same problem. Two tires may look exactly the same, but the specific reasons for the tires to lose air may be entirely different. Establishing the true reason for the tire to go "flat" goes a long way toward correcting the problem. All sinus trouble, sinus headaches, allergy problems, and asthma may "look the same". They are not necessarily caused by the same reason. There can be more than one cause for the problems, exactly as there can be more than one cause for a flat tire. One of the first medical proverbs that I recall is "All that wheezes is not asthma." I might add that all asthma does not always wheeze. Sometimes they just cough or have a hard time breathing at night or present with some other subtle symptom. My point is, however, that all "sinus headaches" will not respond to "sinus medicine". The real problem may be, and often is, further "down the line" at the stomach-esophagus junction. In my patients efforts at relief are much more productive by treating for GERD, especially in people who have tried and failed various other headache remedies. By treating to reduce stomach acid, or in some other measure to reduce the reflux of stomach contents, we are able to effect a truly favorable outcome. Yes, that's right, I am going to give you "stomach medicine" to treat your "allergies", sinus problems, headaches, and to relieve your asthma. One of us is in for a big surprise; you when you get better or me if you don't. This could be the ultimate example of "things are not always as they seem".

Case Study

An 8-year-old female with headaches, respiratory problems, asthma, repeated infections and intermittent severe ear pain. She has never had heartburn. Her history is otherwise unremarkable. Physical examination is likewise unremarkable with the exception of very evident tenderness of the upper abdomen ("solar plexus"). Therapy was initiated with acid blockers. Her dosage was increased when she developed shortness of breath and wheezing while running during the cold, wet month of November. Since then she has remained completely free from ear pain, exercise induced wheezing and shortness of breath. The abdominal tenderness is completely resolved.

Case Study

A 50-year-old male with chronic sinus problems, not known to be allergic to anything and Claritin does not help. Claritin D has helped the most. His sinuses had been troublesome for the last 6 to 7 years. Outcome: The first follow-up 10 days after starting proton pump inhibitors, he noted resolution of sneezing. He still had some throat drainage. At a subsequent appointment, he reports his symptoms for the first time in memory being a 2-3 on a scale of 0 being perfect and 10 the worst they could be. He reports "I am so vastly improved that I don't feel any necessity to use any kind of nose spray or other medication, just the acid blockers." He continues to improve.

VI
WHAT ABOUT HEARTBURN AND MUCOUS?

The most well known symptom of Gastroesophageal Reflux Disease is heartburn. Even when people have heartburn they don't realize the relationship between their "stomach problems" or heartburn, and their sinuses, respiratory, pulmonary, blood pressure, and musculoskeletal conditions. I didn't either until I studied the literature in depth and began to learn about this condition. Like most physicians, I wasn't aware that acid could regurgitate into the esophagus without resulting in heartburn, acid indigestion, or a sour taste in the mouth.

Heartburn is very commonly associated with GERD. So common that most medical practitioners still falsely believe "no heartburn, no GERD". **This is just not true**. The research and modern literature on GERD is crystal clear. It is likely that over half of the people with GERD **do not** have heartburn or digestive tract symptoms of any kind. Many of these people (this is true with heartburn as well) make mucous to protect themselves from their stomach acid. This is where the really interesting things start to happen. Medically we call it *extra esophageal manifestations of GERD*. This means the symptoms we recognize from stomach acid regurgitation are manifest in organs and tissues remote in location from the food tube. Our bodies make mucous to protect the esophagus and respiratory tract from the extremely powerful, caustic chemical hydrochloric acid. This acid is created by the stomach to sterilize the intestinal tract and assist in digestion of our food. The acid "sneaks" past the muscular lower esophageal valve into the bottom of the food tube. The signal that the tissues of the esophagus release when inappropriately exposed to this acid is very intense. The mucous producing tissues are told to make mucous to protect us from the acid being "on the loose" in the esophagus. Mucous producing tissues, not only in the esophagus, but in the sinus cavities, nose, eyes, ears, throat, lungs, and elsewhere, respond to the command by the automatic pilot's signal "make mucous." Miraculously, the body protects itself from its own gastric acid and juices by generating this thick, sticky substance which traps the acid and prevents it from traveling even further from its origin. Other protective mechanisms are involved as well. This is where the sinus trouble starts. The end result is what appears to many individuals as "more mucous than I need." Hence, people awaken (after making acid in their stomach as mother nature intended) with a head, nose, or throat full of mucous, totally unaware that they made the mucous to protect the fragile tissues in their food tube and, if the acid moves further afield, the lungs. The acid "escaped" during sleep, from the stomach, causing the body to put in gear the "mucous machine" to protect other tissues from very serious damage.

It seems that the people who are the best at mucous production have the *most* respiratory symptoms, but demonstrate the *least* amount of damage to their esophagus. If you are good enough at making mucous, you protect your vulnerable tissues so effectively that you *may never get heartburn*. On the other hand, you may make mucous extensively and still get heartburn. At this point, you may think you have two problems; stomach trouble and sinus trouble. It just depends on the individual's response to the escaped stomach acid.

No matter. Research specialists in this area are now realizing the relationship between stomach acid and the "mucous connection." *These concepts are in their infancy.* Your doctor or specialist may not yet be consciously aware of this relationship. We are only now learning about this as a result of using these safe, exceptionally effective, acid reducing medications called *proton pump inhibitors.*

Case Study

A 52-year-old male, with a long standing history of emphysema, intermittent bloody diarrhea, dizziness and depression. His dizziness had gotten to the point that he couldn't drive without taking anxiety medication in anticipation of driving. He was evaluated and under the care of numerous specialists. Aggressive therapy for GERD was instituted and he reports "all of my dizziness is gone, my depression and panic problems have resolved and this is the best I have felt in over twenty years maybe longer!" He remains on GERD therapy and continues to reduce other medications that he has used historically long term for the control of other symptoms. They are no longer necessary.

VII

WHY DOES MY BODY ACT LIKE THIS? I JUST DON'T FEEL RIGHT

You might ask yourself, "Why does the body respond this way?" I am sure that we do not have all the answers yet, but I will give you my understanding. Our internal organs (called visceral organs) are trying to protect themselves as best they can. They are, however, "handicapped". The skin and other external organs are richly invested with sensory nerves to keep the brain fully informed of the environment as we encounter it. It is almost like a spider web of interconnecting nerves that collect this information into the great computer (the brain). The brain processes the information and we react accordingly. Hopefully, we keep ourselves out of harm's way. It's as if there was not enough space internally to wire the visceral organs in the same manner as our skin, lips, and fingers. The end result is less accurate localization of the sensations originating from our internal organs. Examples: jaw, arm, and neck pain originating from the heart; gallbladder problems manifesting as back or chest pain; ear pain from swollen lymph glands in the neck. It seems that many of our internal organs are "hard wired" all on the same circuit. Mother Nature did this to save space. More of these electrical circuits are placed on the *outside* of the body to protect us from the dangerous aspects of the *external* environment. The visceral organs thus do the best they can with the wiring they have.

If my home was set up the same way as the internal organs, then the following scenario might occur. If a hail storm was approaching, I would need to get my car undercover. I would activate the garage door and it would open. The rest of the appliances inside the house on that same space saving circuit would all be activated automatically even though they were *not* what I needed at that time. The end result is that I protected the car, but due to the handicap of the space saving circuit, I activated all the other appliances hooked to the same electrical circuit. The "price" of opening the garage door to allow my car protection from the hail was the "unnecessary" activation of all the other machinery (appliances, lights, oven, fans, etc.) on this electrical circuit. Remember that it worked; my car was saved from damage. The autonomic (automatic) nervous system acts in a similar fashion. The real danger (hail storm) is the gastric acid. When the autonomic nerves are activated (opening the garage door), unwanted results (excessive mucous, choking, muscle spasms, etc.) are encountered as a result of a supreme effort by our bodies to respond to this dangerous insult. All the organs and tissues that got "turned on" were on the same circuit. Maybe I didn't need this type of response, but due to the "space saving" wiring of the electrical circuit, they were activated anyhow.

Our bodies are so good at protecting our esophagus that we may never have a single clue that the problem has, as its origin, "acid indigestion" *without* heartburn. We only see the end result of the activation of protective reflexes as symptoms that are aggravating. As a function of the human element, we have assigned causes as best we can "discover" them. We need to continue on with life despite the inconvenience of sinus trouble, cough, ear pain, and all the other symptoms (nuisance or worse) that we encounter. Hence, as a result of human nature, we develop long lists of causes that are really aggravating cofactors; weather changes, pollen counts, air quality, dust, humidity, pets and dander, temperature changes, perfumes, and infections give us sinus, allergy, and asthma problems. These symptoms turn out to be *complicating* features that make an already troubling situation worse. It acts just like we would expect "allergies" to behave. The only difference is the specific cause and hence the most effective treatment. If you are plagued by these chronic issues of sinus problems, you learn to live with your symptoms and to cope or adapt to them on a day-to-day, hour-to-hour basis the best that you can, never enjoying true good health. Despite avoiding precipitating factors, eating healthy, taking vitamins, using prescription medications, being submitted to numerous tests and so forth, you still feel the same. Usually lousy. In many instances, people with this silent GERD condition, to some extent, have given up on traditional medical care. I certainly understand their frustration. They never really get better or feel good. They go to the doctor, get antibiotics, decongestants, antihistamines, nasal sprays, and the list goes on. In some instances, the therapy may actually make them begin to feel worse. They might think, "Please, if I could just get back to the way I was before this most recent episode, I would be so thankful. I know I wasn't great, but at least I could get by. Now, since this most recent insult and therapy for it, I just seem to be getting worse." This tends to happen over and over. Since only a symptom is being treated and not the true cause of the problem, complete resolution never takes place. The best they <u>ever</u> get is the way they were feeling before *something* made them worse. Individuals often choose alternative remedies to treat their symptoms. The true results may be of little overall favorable effect, but *at least the therapy did NOT* make the person feel worse. The patient often goes from practitioner to practitioner and often crosses specialty lines. All this to be given the same therapies with the same poor results, i.e., another course of the latest antibiotic; a different decongestant; a new kind of nose spray, but to no avail. Sound familiar?

To illustrate this situation, several examples come to mind. One in particular was an "experimental study" in children ages 2-18 where 30 consecutive patients were referred to a specialty center for chronic sinusitis . All of these youngsters had failed repeated therapies with multiple antibiotics and had exhausted all sinus remedies. They thus ended up in this particular study.

Researchers were looking for any answer they could find. They anticipated a 5% incidence of GERD. By testing, using our most current technologies, they were able to establish that over 60% of these youngsters were suffering from GERD. This brings us back to the concept that I speak of elsewhere in the book, what I call a "treat then test" model of therapeutic challenge. I expect that even more than 60% of these kids would have responded if treated for GERD.

Perhaps this is the right time for me to mention that other conditions can be associated with silent atypical GERD. The surgical literature reflects a high incidence of gallstones associated with classic GERD at 38%. The occurrence of gallstones, pre-gallstones, and gallbladder problems appears to be extremely common. Though I have no formal statistics, my suspicion is over 50% of people who experience GERD are harboring gallbladder problems. The same factors that result in GERD symptoms cause chronic muscle spasms at the outlet to the gallbladder. This causes obstruction of bile. With stagnation of the gallbladder contents, gallbladder disease ensues. All of this as a direct result of protecting ourselves from the stomach acid. It also appears that sleep disturbances are particularly common in GERD patients. In some instances, these proposed GERD mechanisms interfere with normal breathing patterns and thus result in disrupted sleep. Poor quality sleep, for any reason, results in daytime fatigue. The condition of Sleep Apnea can be a *result* of the stomach contents moving up into the esophagus. Sleep Apnea, by its very nature, causes the tendency to draw stomach contents into the esophagus as a consequence of attempting to inhale air into the lungs. When this happens, it looks and acts like GERD. I am only mentioning these conditions in passing to help you realize that other conditions can mimic or complicate the diagnosis of GERD.

VIII
MORE MUCOUS THAN I NEED... NOTHING EVER WORKS ON ME

The specialists that deal in this area of the gastrointestinal tract discuss four possible mechanisms involved in GERD.

1) Too much acid. This, in many ways, is the easiest to treat because we have the most effective medications of all the remedies at our disposal. The medications called *proton pump inhibitors* have the ability to reduce the amount of stomach acid produced. They are extremely safe, effective, and constitute the most successful pharmacologic intervention in GERD. They *never* eradicate hydrochloric acid production completely (This has **nothing** to do with any other acids in the body. They remain unchanged and are not part of this issue.)

2) The "supersensitive" esophagus. This means that my personal sensitivity to hot dishes from the dishwasher is so great that I have to wait until they cool off before I can handle them. My wife is able to handle them while they are still hot. They don't hurt her hands like they do mine.

The implication is that even a person who makes what is considered to be a normal amount of hydrochloric acid can trigger this whole process when the acid comes into contact with the *supersensitive food tube*. In some individuals, even very tiny amounts of gastric juice or stomach acid leaking into the esophagus can cause an overwhelming, full-blown, "mucous response".

3) Acid entrapment in the food tube. In this situation, the esophagus is not overly sensitive, nor is there an unusually strong quality to the stomach acid. A portion of the stomach acid gets trapped in the lower section of the food tube (it is not supposed to be there). This causes prolonged contact with the lining of the esophagus. When this happens, the body's internal alarms become activated. Even small amounts of acid can cause this response. As well, a whole physiological chain of events that we utilize in an attempt to soothe and protect the lining of the food tube are initiated thru the autonomic nervous system.*

4) Gastric back-up. Another possibility is that the bottom valve at the outlet of the stomach (the pyloric valve) goes into spasm or does not relax properly. This causes a back up of gastric contents very similar to the situation that arises when your drain pipe becomes plugged. You can visualize this situation by holding a tube of toothpaste out in front of you with the top pointed toward the ceiling. When you remove the cap from the tube of toothpaste and squeeze mid-tube, the toothpaste squirts toward the ceiling in the path of least resistance. In some manner or another, this seems to be the most consistent pattern that we encounter in people with GERD.

*The vagus nerve is intimately involved.

POSSIBLE MECHANISMS OF GERD

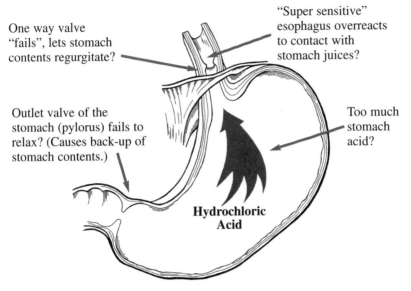

One way valve "fails", lets stomach contents regurgitate?

"Super sensitive" esophagus overreacts to contact with stomach juices?

Outlet valve of the stomach (pylorus) fails to relax? (Causes back-up of stomach contents.)

Too much stomach acid?

Hydrochloric Acid

FACTS ABOUT GERD

1. Over 50% of GERD patients **DO NOT** have heartburn.

2. Throat clearing and headache, closely followed by cough and nasal congestion occur in over 50% of patients with GERD.

3. GERD is not recognized in non-industrialized countries.

4. Studies document 90% of chronic asthma patients have GERD.

5. Reducing stomach acid production does not impair digestion.

6. Over 66% of allergy patients **WILL NOT** respond to antihistamines or allergy therapy.

7. Proton pump inhibitors **DO NOT** have any effect on other acids in the body (uric acid, lactic acid, carbonic acid, etc.)

8. Proton pump inhibitors **DO NOT** eliminate stomach acid.

WHAT IS THE GOAL OF TREATMENT IN GERD?

The goal of treatment is to reduce the amount of stomach acid "backing up" into the esophagus. Medication may be necessary to relieve symptoms and heal any damage to the esophagus.

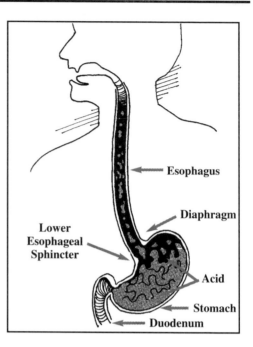

To further complicate GERD problems, we make acid both when we sleep and when we eat. At this point in time, we know that we can help reduce the acid associated with meals, but we have very little influence or ability to decrease the amount of acid we make while we sleep.

In today's age of highly effective pharmaceutical products, we now have very safe medications which have significant control over how much or how strong the body makes the hydrochloric acid in the stomach at mealtime. We've had these potent acid inhibitors for over a decade in regular clinical use. These medications do not prevent all stomach acid production. They just reduce it. Enough acid is made while we sleep to sterilize the intestinal tract and assist in digestion. Since the medications we have at our disposal inhibit the amount of acid made in conjunction with meals, they lower the total amount of acid made on a daily basis. This reduces the "load" of acid that our esophagus may be exposed to during the day and especially at night. It helps symptoms by making the acid in the gastric juices more bland, while not eliminating acid entirely.

In researching the effects of these medications on GERD, results that show improvement in ear, nose, and throat symptoms (versus the more typical symptoms of heartburn or regurgitation) ***REQUIRE MORE POTENT ACID SUPPRESSION*** for a longer duration of treatment. This means a higher dose of medicine for days, weeks or months before sinus or other extra esophageal symptoms remit. Hence, heartburn is easier to eradicate than sinus trouble. Heartburn often responds almost immediately to just one capsule a day. It's "easy" to control heartburn compared to sinus troubles. Sinus-type respiratory problems are more resistant or impossible to resolve on the lower heartburn control doses of acid blocker therapy. This means sticking to the commitment of ongoing therapy and not assuming the "Nothing ever works for me. This doesn't either" philosophy.

While the medicine I have mentioned offers significant control over GERD, lifestyle and dietary changes are of potential benefit. The treatments your family members have had in the past for hiatal hernia are almost identical with the recommendations that we have at this time for GERD. They are consistent with the purported mechanisms causing GERD. Remember, the end result is stomach contents escaping upward past the muscular one-way valve at the bottom of the food tube and ending up where they are unwelcome. Recommended changes:

1. Raise the head of the bed six inches so that gravity is working in your favor. I have used books, wooden blocks, bricks, plastic bed risers and car jacks. Cushions or extra pillows placed between the mattress and box springs have also been helpful. This helps to keep the gastric contents below the level of the gastroesophageal (stomach-food tube) junction. If you slide down too much in bed, then reduce the height. Pillows under your head may kink the food tube and are

not a good alternative. A foam wedge on or under the mattress is an option. Waterbeds are strongly discouraged.

2. Avoid eating or filling your stomach 2-3 hours before lying down in order to help decrease back pressure on the valve at the top of your stomach.

3. Avoid foods that decrease the ability of the lower esophageal valve (the area where the esophagus and the stomach join) to squeeze shut. Mints, chocolate, caffeine, and even decaffeinated coffee, as well as, some prescription medications, all seem to decrease the ability of the valve to function effectively.

4. Avoid tight-fitting clothing. It acts like a tourniquet on your bowel and causes a low grade obstruction to the flow of intestinal contents.

5. If you have a choice, lying on your left side helps your body contain acid in the stomach. It is almost as effective as raising the head of your bed on six-inch blocks.

6. Other common sense remedies: avoiding prolonged sitting; reducing weight; correcting sedentary lifestyles; limiting excessive alcohol, acidic foods, high-fat diet, and tobacco all seem helpful. These all play some role in the evolution and persistence of acid related disorders.

At first glance, I know it seems hard to believe that your sore throat in the morning when you awaken (or neck ache, or ear pain, or the choking spell, or the runny nose, or a lot of other symptoms) could possibly be a response to the acid traveling up into your food tube the night before. Many people ask, "Why no discomfort? Why no heartburn or belching or taste of acid in my mouth?" I think of it like this. If your "fire department" (mucous making tissue) is in good repair and has plenty of reserve supplies, you can be very responsive to the "fire alarm" from your body. The *majority* of people are able to prevent heartburn by natural mechanisms (such as swelling of tissues, making mucous and/or muscle spasms) to trap the escaped gastric juices. These processes prevent acid from moving further upstream once they have already violated the barrier of the valve.[2] Meanwhile, the acid triggers unwanted and often "excessive" mucous. Your body (the fire department) responds to the "fire alarm" of acid in the food tube successfully. So successfully that you neutralize the acid **WITHOUT GETTING HEARTBURN**. Your esophagus says, "thank you," but your sinuses say, "Where did all this phlegm come from?" And now you know, as Paul Harvey, the radio personality, would say, "the rest of the story."

[2] The check valve at the bottom of the esophagus is a muscular ring that allows food and drink to pass into the stomach as part of the complex swallowing mechanism. It is intended to function as a one-way barrier to regurgitation. Medically, it is dubbed the "Lower Esophageal Sphincter" (LES).

Case Study

   A long standing, female patient, 62 years old, with a chronic history of migraine headaches, uncontrolled runny nose, upper respiratory allergies, high blood pressure and elevated cholesterol. The only thing that ever helped her headaches were "sinus/allergy medications". Institution of GERD therapy has resulted in dramatic improvement. The patient states, "I am doing really good." Her blood pressure, which was nearly impossible to control in the past, has normalized at 110/60. The headaches are gone. She is on less medicine then she has ever taken before with improved results. As of this date she still has "minor" trouble with "a runny nose".

IX
THE ACID-MUCOUS
CONNECTION

In my opinion, here is what occurs. NOTE: It is all about stomach acid violating the valve at the top of the stomach and coming in contact with the lining of the food tube. (For sake of simplification and clarification, it is technically the contents of the stomach that we are talking about here, but for the sake of simplicity and understanding I will generally refer to the gastric contents as acid or stomach acid.)

It is well known that the stomach makes hydrochloric acid. It is poorly appreciated, however, that the intensity and strength of the stomach acid is *dangerous* to our own tissues. Surgeons and anesthesia doctors know of this danger and forbid you to eat or drink anything the night before surgery to decrease the amount, and therefore, the likelihood, of stomach acid going from your stomach via the esophagus into your lungs or respiratory tract at the time of your surgery

Mother Nature made the lining of the stomach with the unique ability to protect itself from this caustic material, the "industrial strength" hydrochloric acid that the stomach itself makes. This is not your ordinary type of acid that occurs in nature like vinegar (acetic acid) or orange juice (citric acid). This is *really* strong acid. Stronger than battery acid. Everything is fine and in harmony as long as the acid stays in the stomach as planned. It is only when the acid travels "upstream" from the stomach into the food tube that some really fascinating things begin to happen. In the most basic terms, the valve (LES) fails to contain the acid within the stomach, hence, with the failure of the valve, people make mucous to protect their food tube from this inordinately powerful agent. The acid moves from the stomach into the food tube inappropriately. The food tube senses the imminent danger from such a harsh, corrosive substance. It sends out signals that encourages the esophagus and respiratory tract to make mucous to defend themselves. Miraculously, the body, by making mucous and other protective mechanisms, defends itself from the gastric acid. Unfortunately, the other mucous producing tissues of the body are stimulated by the intensity of this signal and the end result is what appears to the individual as "more mucous than I need."

Perhaps we could think of it this way. Suppose that your finger was about to touch a red hot burner on the stove. Your body would protect itself with an involuntary reflex; that of an avoidance mechanism, i.e., you would instantly pull your finger away automatically, without conscious thought. Quite obviously, it is not possible for your esophagus to use the same mechanism, i.e., an avoidance reflex to protect itself from the stomach acid. Nevertheless, in the same manner that your body protected you from the hot burner on the stove, your esophagus uses automatic reflex mechanisms to protect you from the acidic contents that come in contact with the fragile lining of the esophagus.

Now remember, this acid is unbelievably strong, so strong it cannot be stored in ordinary metal containers because it will eat its way through. It will easily dissolve tinfoil. It's usually stored in glass or crock. Your body, with its amazing ability to adapt, is able to protect itself from this life threatening, acid-induced danger. There is a price to pay for this protection. Your tissues have to compensate with the results of this extreme mucous production throughout the rest of your body. Your body purposefully neglects other "needs" to protect your food tube and lungs from the stomach acid.

Let's try some common sense. If you were the esophagus and you were being attacked by a very harsh chemical, how could you protect yourself? One of the defense mechanisms at your disposal would be the ability to make what, at times, seems like an endless supply of mucous. Also you have at your disposal a message to leak tissue fluid (this is how blisters are generated.) Another part of the alarm message says to tissues *SWELL UP* (sprained ankle for example). If the hollow esophagus squeezes down hard (muscle spasm), it prevents the further upward movement of foreign gastric contents. As a matter of fact, these protective mechanisms are so effective that a *majority* of people who experience reflux or acid reflux or GERD, *never have heartburn*! One result is lots of mucous, not only in your esophagus, but elsewhere, in your eyes, ears, nose, throat, etc. In some ways, the better you are at these protective mechanisms, the less likely you are to realize that the primary problem is from the acid escaping from the stomach.

Remember all of those times that you just knew that it was because your sick child was "swallowing all of that mucous" that his stomach became upset, causing him to start vomiting? Please consider that it's the other way around. It all starts in your child's esophagus. Your child's body is making mucous to protect itself from prolonged exposure to the stomach acid up in the esophagus. One of the signs of excessive stomach acid is vomiting. The mucous, as one of its primary goals, has the ability to trap the acid in order to prevent it from traveling and causing further damage. In so doing, this mucous not only detains hydrochloric acid, but it also traps allergy particles, respiratory infections and foreign substances. This results in recurrent infections, ear problems, allergy symptoms and more.

Your child's vomiting may result because he or she has something wrong at the stomach/food tube junction; the mucous is created within their bodies because they are trying to protect themselves from the escaped stomach acid. The respiratory symptoms are an example of how a person acts and feels when they have "too much" mucous, more than they need in their respiratory tract. It is a result of their bodies' all out responses to successfully trap and neutralize the acid that has escaped from the stomach. The immune system is weakened because its resources are drained to make mucous and protect against the acid. The child ends up with respiratory infections, ear problems and fevers, which we treat. It all recurs because we haven't identified and treated the cause, i.e., escaped stomach acid.

The autonomic nervous system (this is Mother Natures version of the automatic pilot) is a marvelous, remarkable setup. We all know about the "fight or flight" response. Someone or something threatens you. Your body, through the autonomic nervous system, prepares you to protect yourself by running away *fast* or getting super strong to fight. All of this in order to survive the perceived threat. This is how a single person rights an overturned vehicle showing "super-human" strength to save another's life. It is done by releasing chemicals (messengers if you will) via nerves and the bloodstream to alert and ready your *entire* body for the challenge your brain recognizes. In the same manner, your *internal* environment is being constantly monitored for "threats". Your body consistently monitors your blood pressure, sugar levels, oxygen levels, etc. Through the autonomic nervous system, these parameters are being constantly evaluated, controlled and corrected by the release of chemical messengers.

The end result is protection of the esophagus at your own "expense". You "pay" for this protection from hydrochloric acid with repeated respiratory infections, cough, ear infections, ear pain, bronchitis, asthma, sore throats, swollen glands in the neck, or some combination of these or other symptoms. This response to escaped stomach acid makes some people feel fatigued, rundown, "stressed out" and cranky! They often feel like their immune system is weak. No amount of healthy foods, vitamins, herbs, or aerobic exercise, despite wonderful intentions, will reverse or correct the problems. All of these well-conceived remedies give less than complete or satisfactory results. Treating the underlying "cause" (escaped stomach contents) helps to relieve a huge variety of "effects".

THE ACID-MUCOUS CONNECTION

Stomach acid escapes upward into the lower food tube. The vagus nerve (Autonomic Nervous System) is triggered to protect the delicate tissues of the esophagus, throat and lungs from the corrosive effects of the gastric secretions.

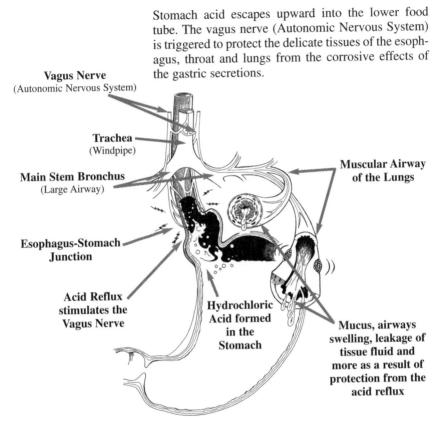

Vagus Nerve
(Autonomic Nervous System)

Trachea
(Windpipe)

Main Stem Bronchus
(Large Airway)

**Muscular Airway
of the Lungs**

**Esophagus-Stomach
Junction**

**Acid Reflux
stimulates the
Vagus Nerve**

**Hydrochloric
Acid formed
in the
Stomach**

**Mucus, airways
swelling, leakage of
tissue fluid and
more as a result of
protection from the
acid reflux**

Comments from Sharon K.

Since I have been under treatment for GERD I have seen many improvements in my quality of life. I used to have a major sinus infection two or more times per year. I have not had a major problem since my treatment began and we found the medication and dosage that I reacted to. I sleep better, don't burp all the time, and have adjusted to my new self. So much that it's hard to remember what it used to be like. I have found out that, just because that's the way my body has always reacted, doesn't mean it can't change. My only regret is that I did not take my situation as one that could be addressed with the proper medication and care. Thank you so much for having the 'grit' to hang in there with me.

X
HOW DO I GET BETTER?

Number one on the list is to realize that even in the absence of heartburn, your problems may be the result of gastroesophageal reflux. Educate yourself about this condition. Become knowledgeable and familiar with the various aspects of this problem. Go to your family doctor and ask them to consider this as a possibility in your differential diagnosis. These are new concepts. Your healthcare provider (the Medicare name for physician and surgeon) will know about GERD. The majority of doctors are unaware of the prevalence of silent GERD. The most widely disseminated guidelines for treatment are for traditional GERD and therapy is directed at heartburn control. Successful treatment of respiratory symptoms requires increased amounts of medication. Many prescription insurance providers base your pharmacy benefits on these conventional guidelines. In some instances they make variations in the form of increased dosages a reason to refuse to pay for your medication. The vast majority of physicians are unaware of this impending dilemma. The therapy guidelines for silent GERD are not yet completely developed or uniformly acknowledged. It takes incredible energy, resources, and tenacity to educate and convert some parts of this healthcare system. Your doctor is not responsible for this superimposed framework of financial constraints. In some instances, your doctor will be put at financial retribution. The insurance providers will take money away for prescribing this "not yet in the cookbook" therapy.

Hence, not every doctor I talk to is as excited about this as I am. That's partly why I'm writing this book. I am trying to help you, as a patient, to understand "why" and what you may be up against in order to get better. Oftentimes providers will say, "Oh no. We couldn't give you this medicine without doing tests." I say, "Why not? *YOU MIGHT GET BETTER*." Especially if you have unsuccessfully tried other therapies. Dr. Ricther, and Dr. Fass, and others agree. The medication is safe. There are few drug interactions. The treatment is well tolerated. Testing can be complex and <u>not</u> reliable. The tests can be misleading to the point of saying, "You don't have GERD," when, in fact, you really do since a therapeutic trial of proton pump inhibitors gives *TOTAL RELIEF*. No harm comes to you from the medication if you don't have GERD. Your symptoms will remain unchanged. For those who do suffer from GERD, especially in the early stages of treatment, when you stop the medicine, your symptoms almost always reappear quickly. You take the medicine for a defined period of time (one week, two weeks, one month, etc.) and if you get enough medicine, with luck, you get better. I mean *ALL BETTER*. This medication is so safe, it is expected to go "over the counter" soon. No prescription will be necessary.

If you do respond favorably, that's when the challenges really begin: Why do I have this? What tests do I need to have done? How should I treat this short-term? Long term? Should I have surgery? What does this mean for my family history? Will my insurance pay for this medication? For surgery? What if they don't? What might happen in the future if I don't stay on therapy? I don't have all of the answers to these and other questions. I just know that I regularly see people *get all better when treated*. Here's a hint. If you do get to TRY this therapy, *pay attention* and keep track because other, totally unexpected problems are going to disappear. My opinion is that, at the very least, you deserve to know whether GERD plays a role in your illness. My experience tells me this is very common. It "happened" to *both* my daughters. They are better and nothing else ever helped!

The more remedies you have tried and **FAILED**, the more likely it is that GERD plays a role in your condition. If the primary care provider can't help you, ask or seek out a *knowledgeable* ENT physician (otolaryngologist) to evaluate you. Sometimes informed gastroenterologists, internists, pediatricians or general surgeons will be willing to help you as well. No matter what the specialty, your doctor won't recognize this condition for what it really is if he/she is not aware of these newer concepts that are not as yet in the classical medical textbooks.

It may be necessary for you to *educate* your doctor or enlighten your specialist in regard to this condition. The information is out there. It's available, but it takes an especially informed, caring, patient and dedicated doctor to work with you and fight for you to be able to secure the expensive medication necessary to confirm and treat this condition. Someone has to go "outside the box" as your advocate until this syndrome or disease is more widely acknowledged.

In this book, you will find a list of symptoms that I use to assist me if I suspect this diagnosis. The symptoms don't need to be troublesome, *only present*, to be of significance. The symptom sheet needs to be completed from the standpoint, "I will mark this even though I already know why I have this symptom." Example: " I won't mark sneezing . That's just from my allergies and I don't sneeze unless I am around a certain breed of cat, so I don't need to worry about that–**WRONG**–*mark it*. Especially if *you have GERD*, you have spent a lifetime making excuses (that are not your fault) for certain symptoms.

The more medical problems you have or have had that just don't respond dramatically to the wonderfully effective medications that we now have suggests to me something else is causing those symptoms.

You might say, "Doctor, test me to see if I have GERD." This brings up an issue that sometimes confuses patients and practitioners alike. We don't have testing that is sensitive enough to find *all* the folks who have this problem. Remember the children in the "experimental study" in Chapter Seven. I suspect they *all* had GERD. I hope they were treated successfully. Because the medication is so safe and, in most cases, so effective, most often we **TREAT** first and monitor closely to look for resolution of signs and symptoms. The treatment is the "test"; this is called a "GI stress test". We treat you, in this case with a strong dose of medication and, if you get better, it means you had "too much acid" as the cause of your symptoms. It results in a "treat then test" paradigm. Many doctors seem hesitant to adopt this model of disease diagnosis. They aren't familiar with the relationships in silent, atypical GERD. They have been trained to confirm the diagnosis by evidence based on proven testing before initiating therapy. I have had another doctor tell my patient after visualizing their esophagus, "Your food tube is healthy. You don't need that medicine." The statement should be qualified by saying, "You don't need that medicine to *heal* your food tube. It doesn't show any injury, **BUT** your doctor is giving you the right medicine to control your *symptoms* that results in keeping your food tube healthy, free from being injured by the hydrochloric acid." Surgeons and bowel specialists tend to be the most inclined in this line of thought. They look for injured tissue. They are accustomed to "fixing" damaged or "broken" tissues. In most of the cases I see, I treat a protective reflex, the cause of which is *reflux* of stomach contents. The end result is no damage to the tissues of the esophagus from the regurgitation of the stomach contents, only because your body is so *good* at protecting itself! In silent GERD, if you look for damaged tissues in the esophagus to prove the diagnosis, you will be disappointed and never get better. We treat silent GERD and your body turns off the "protective reflex" and you get better.

A thirty-year-old woman struggled with ear pain, sore throats, asthma and neck pain. Over a four month period recently, she had six courses of antibiotics, plus her regular allergy and asthma medicine. She couldn't get well. She was sent to the allergy specialist. He couldn't help. Next she went to the gastroenterologist, specifically for the investigation of GERD. She did everything asked of her, including invasive testing and leaving a tube down her nose into her esophagus to the level near her stomach for a twenty-four hour period in order to measure the escaped acid. They told her, "You do not appear to have GERD. Sorry, no treatment." At this point I became involved. In spite of the test results, I suggested proton pump inhibitor medication to reduce stomach acid production. Within days, she was improved and within a couple of months or less, she was "perfect". So perfect that she no longer takes *any* allergy or sinus medication at all. She continues to take proton pump inhibitors to maintain her good health.

The emphasis here is therapy to confirm the *real cause* of symptoms. The medicine is so safe, so effective, and the condition of the extraesophageal manifestations of GERD is so difficult to confirm, using our current diagnostic techniques that we need a high index of suspicion regarding the problem. To be successful, the doctor needs the willingness to use the medication, in high doses if necessary, to establish the diagnosis.

The less heartburn a person has, including *no* heartburn at all, the higher the dose of the medication they are likely to *need* to establish and treat this condition. This may seem "backwards", but it is true. Using the medication in this manner is called "gastrointestinal stress test" (GI stress test), therapeutic challenge or empiric therapy.

To treat peptic ulcers and most individuals' heartburn, one pill is *extraordinarily effective*. So effective, that physicians and other providers have grown accustomed to the wonderfully successful results with heartburn eradication by taking just one pill or even an occasional dose. The dose to control extraesophageal GERD symptoms is almost always higher. I often put a person on one or two pills or capsules of proton pump inhibitors twice a day before meals (after a single test dose of one pill to see how they tolerate the medicine). The most common side effects[3] are upset stomach, diarrhea, or headache. I ask them to come back in a fortnight and then we reevaluate. I have not gotten every single person better, **BUT** there have been overwhelmingly favorable results in the majority of people.

GERD is a long term, chronic condition and the best statistics we have (for erosive esophagitis) at this time show 80% of GERD patients will relapse within six months of discontinuation of therapy. These statistics may not apply because they almost always use heartburn relief as a parameter. The only measurable effect on the body with proton pump inhibitors is decreased secretion of hydrochloric acid. Therefore, this medication is believed to be safe. In the beginning, there was concern about stomach cancer or stomach tumors on a *theoretical basis*. After the huge popularity of these pharmaceutical agents became apparent, the safety issues seemed even of less concern. Why? When a medication is *widely* used (#1 prescription in the USA) flaws, side effects, previously unknown effects, drug interactions, fatalities, may all become apparent early on in a drug's history. If a new medication is used by only a "few" patients, it could be months or years before enough experiences are encountered to uncover these tendencies. I don't like to use "new" drugs, no matter how good they seem. I'd rather they be in general use first. When I buy a car, I'd rather buy a model that has already been in production and driven by the public. They discover the flaws. The proton pump inhibitors were introduced in the 1980's. They proved immediately to be a wonderful alternative to radical surgery to remove the stomach of individuals with a rare "super acid production" condition known as Zollinger-Ellison Syndrome. This condition requires very high doses of proton pump inhibitors for the duration of their lives. The medication has stood the test of time. In these individuals, high doses of proton pump inhibitors have been in use continuously for over fifteen years. There have been no adverse, unan-

---

[3] Side effects are uncommon and occur in less than 3% of individuals.

ticipated effects. The major criticism is expense–$3.00 per dose or more.

An alternative to medication in GERD is surgery at the junction of the food tube and stomach, called a "stomach-esophagus wrap" (Nissen Fundoplication) through the telescope (laparoscope). The upper portion of the stomach is used to encircle the lower esophagus. The intent is to restore competency to the LES valve.*

Certainly, the means have to justify the end result i.e., "the punishment should fit the crime." One surgeon told my patient, "I wouldn't do surgery on your stomach just because you have a runny nose." I agree wholeheartedly, *but* if that person had 2-4 episodes a year of pus-producing, high fever, impacted sinusitis with the resultant danger of brain abscess, bloodstream infection and death, I wouldn't cross surgery off the list. I would find a more enlightened surgeon.

In my experience, the more therapies that you have tried and failed; the more times you have been told, "It's all in your head," the more frustrated you are with traditional medicine, the more likely you are to have, as a source of your health problems, GERD or silent GERD.

Good luck to you in finding a cause and getting healthy! It won't automatically be easy. To be successful you will need to be persistent, educated, patient, and willing to tolerate the ignorance (lack of knowledge) of many insurance companies, mail order pharmaceutical suppliers, doctors, nurses, and even medical specialists in this field. Your body harbors the necessary elements for good health. By listening carefully to what your body is telling us, we can alleviate symptoms by identifying the cause, not just treating the noxious symptoms. We assist your body by reducing the acidic content of the gastric juice. Your body does the rest. *"WITHIN THE BODY THERE LIES A CURE."*™

---

*An exciting new alternative is just now becoming available. Sutures can now be placed *inside* the esophagus using a flexible telescope down the throat. This eliminates the need to cut skin or tissue.

APPENDIX

PHYSICAL SIGNS OF GERD

Should your personal physician chose to pursue this approach to your illness, you may wish to share my observations.
Kurt A. Barrett, D.O.

Physical signs associated with SNERD (silent, non-erosive, gastroesophageal reflux disorder) are anecdotal, but appear with impressive frequency. If present, they tend to strongly confirm the diagnosis. Their absence (or remission) are of little consequence unless correlation of symptom resolution is considered in the latter circumstances. These findings include a yellow tinge to the normal sparkling clear tympanic membrane (ear drum) and can be unilateral, bilateral, or not evident at all. This, I believe, is representative of the presence of mucous in abnormal amounts and in atypical locations. At times, ear drums actually weep, allowing secretions to accumulate in the ear canal in the absence of infection or disruption of the tympanic membrane.

In the nares impressive, spherical swelling of the inferior turbinate can be identified either bilaterally, or oftentimes unilaterally. This virtually always recedes with therapy and hence assumes a normal appearance. The disease state is often characterized by turbinate engorgement, not infrequently to the point of total occlusion, of the air passageways. The edematous engorged inferior turbinate tissue resembles the appearance anatomically of engorged external hemorrhoids. Copious amounts of mucous with or without purulence (pus) is not an unexpected finding in association with the openings to the sinuses. In a significant percentage of patients the uvula or the uvular portion of the soft pallet appears characteristically abnormal. These changes may be subtle, but in my experience as I become accustomed to recognizing these changes, they appear rather characteristic. The uvula can be distorted by what I would call "soft", non-engorged, pale appearing, edematous swollen tissues. The uvula may be enlarged in any of its dimensions, be that diameter or girth, as opposed to the length. The total volume of the uvula, if excessive at the initiation of therapy, virtually always recedes dramatically in size when therapy is completely successful. At other times, the uvula will appear tense, ruborous, edematous and enlarged implying congested interstitial tissues Occasionally, there will be an accompanying stream of tenacious mucous. Quite often, the posterior pharynx will show a "scalloped" appearance with reddened hypertrophied lymphoid tissue interspersed with threads, strands and streams of adherent mucous. The tonsils and the tonsillar pillars may be enlarged or engorged or normal in appearance. If there is an extensive absence of teeth, oftentimes the posterior aspect of the dental distribution is the most heavily involved (the molars). Occasionally, caries of an extensive nature will be noted in between all front, back, upper and lower teeth as a progression to total decalcification, periodontal disease and loss of most, if not all, teeth. Again, in my personal experience, if a characteristic odor is present, it is diagnostic. It is what I identify as halitosis. If present, it is exclusively associated with patients experiencing some form of reflux. The reflux causes mucous to adhere to dental structures. A bacteria, Streptococcus mucans, grows in the mucous and results in this special, foul odor. Dental caries ("cavities") often follow.

Upper abdominal and sternal tenderness is common and can involve specific segments of the sternum, the entire sternum, the xyphoid process or the immediate adjacent epigastric tissues.

The absence of tenderness is of little clinical value. The presence of tenderness (in the absence of any explained phenomenon such as trauma, surgery, etc.) is uniquely correlated with gastroesophageal reflux.

9 Steps To Relieving GERD Symptoms.

1. Avoid Foods If They Cause Symptoms

Avoid these foods if they aggravate symptoms: chocolate, mints, coffee, tea, colas, and alcoholic beverages, spicy and fatty foods, tomato and citrus juices (such as grapefruit and orange juices).

2. Limit Coffee

Limit your coffee (or other caffeine-containing beverages) intake to 2-3 cups per day.

3. Do Not Lie Down For Two Hours After Eating

Allow gravity to work. Also, bend at the knees instead of bending over at the waist to pick up things.

4. Eat Smaller Meals

Do not overfill your stomach.

5. Lose Weight

Excess weight can increase the pressure that is constantly placed on your stomach. The smallest amount of weight loss can help.

6. Antacids
Antacids can be helpful if taken at bedtime and 30-60 minutes after meals.

7. Avoid Tight Clothing
Tight pants, belts or girdles can increase the amount of pressure on the abdomen.

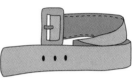

8. Stop Smoking
If you think your can't stop, decreasing the number of cigarettes you smoke may help.

9. Bed Blocks
Elevate the head of your bed 2-6 inches with bricks or wood blocks. Do not use extra pillows, using a foam wedge beneath the upper half of the body is an alternative.

BIBLIOGRAPHY

Books

Castell, Donald O., M.D., Richter, Joel E., M.D., *The Esophagus, Third Edition,* Lipppincott, Williams, & Wilkins, 1999

Hildreth, Arthur Grant, D.O., *The Lengthening Shadow of Dr. Andrew Taylor Still,* Simpson Printing Company, 1938

Modlin, Irvin M., M.D., PhD., and Sachs, George, M.D., *Acid Related Diseases,* Schnetzter-Verlay Gmbh Konstanz, 1998

Wolfe, M. Michael, M.D.,and Nesi, Thomas, *The Fire Inside,* W.W. Norton, 1996

Periodicals

Clouse, R.E., *Psychiatric Disorders in Patients with Esophageal Disease,* Medical Clinics, North America, September 1991

Freston, James W., *Long Term Acid Control and Proton Pump Inhibitors: Interactions and Safety Issues in Perspective,* "The American Journal of Gastroenterology," Vol 92, No. 419

Gaynor, E.B., *Otolaryngologic Manifestations of Gastroesophageal Reflux,* "The American Journal of Gastroenterology," July 1991

Israel, David M. and Hassoll, Eric, *Omeprazole and Other Proton Pump Inhibitors: Pharmacology, Efficacy, and Safety, with Special Reference to Use in Children,* "Journal of Pediatric Gastroenterology and Nutrition," November 1998

Majica, V.R. and Rao, S.S., *Recognizing Atypical Manifestations of GERD. Asthma, Chest Pain, and Otolaryngologic Disorders May be Due to Reflux.,* "Postgraduate Medicine," January 1999

Ours, Tina M., and Richter, Joel E., M.D., *Evaluating Chronic Cough: Is Reflux the Cause?,* "The Journal of Respiratory Diseases," Vol. 21, No. 11, November 2000

Phipps, C.D., Wood, W.E., Gibson, W.S., Cochran, W.J., *Gastroesophageal Reflux Contributing to Chronic Sinus Disease in Children: A Prospective Analysis,* "Arch Otolaryngal Head Neck Surgery 2000"; 126: 831-836

Richter, J.E., M.D., *Gastroesophageal Reflux Disease and Asthma: The Two are Directly Related,* "The American Journal of Medicine," March 6, 2000

Theodoropoulos, M.D, Demetrios S., and Ledford.M.D., Dennis, *Is GERD a Factor in Your Patient's Asthma?,* "The Journal of Respiratory Diseases," Vol. 21, No. 4, April 2000

Thjodleifsson, M.D., and Jonsson, Palmi V., *Management of Gastroesophageal Reflux Disease in the Elderly Patient,* "Clinical Geriatrics," Vol. 9, No. 6, May 2001

Walters, Jken, et al, *The Use of Omeprazole in the Pediatric Population,* "The Annals of Pharmacotherapy," April 1998, Vol. 32

Other

Interactive Teleconference Workshop
Fass, M.D., Ronnie, Director, G.I. Motility Laboratory, Southern Arizona VA Healthcare System, *Extraesophageal Manifestations of GERD,* 2001

Continuing Education Monograph
Robinson, M.D., Malcolm and Horn, John R., *Acid Suppression Update: Advances in Therapy with Proton Pump Inhibitors,* August 1, 2000

Personal Communication (Letter)
Reinhardt, M.D., Robert W., *Allergy Screening Program,* January 17, 2001, Pharmacia Corporation

News Brief
Hicks, Douglas PhD. Voice Center, Speech Language Professor, Cleveland Clinic's Department of Otolaryngology and Communicative Disorders, *Collaboration Aimed at Understanding Reflux, 2000*

Mayo Clinical Update
Endoscopic Fundoplication for Gastroesophageal Reflux Disease, Vol. 16, No. 3, 2000

Pathways
Case Studies in GERD Management, February 28, 2000, Richter, Joel E., M.D., et al, The Cleveland Clinic Foundation.